BENJAMIN D. AUTHOR

OPEN SES●A●ME

UNLOCKING THE HIDDEN DOORS WITHIN OURSELVES

© 2020 Benjamin D Author
Book ISBN 978-1-7339949-4-1
Published By: Great Lineage Publishing Company

Scripture quotations are taken from the Holy Bible,
New Living Translation, copyright © 1996, 2004, 2015
by Tyndale House Foundation. Used by permission
of Tyndale House Publishers, Inc., Carol Stream,
Illinois 60188. All rights reserved.

Scripture taken from the New King James Version®.
Copyright © 1982 by Thomas Nelson.
Used by permission. All rights reserved.

Cover and interior layout and design by
Priceless Digital Media.

DEDICATION

I am dedicating *Open Sesame* to the dedicated men and women who have decided to strive for a lifelong relationship with their spouses and spouses-to-be and not the "same ol', roll-of-the-dice" relationship that has become so common to the world today. My prayer is that this book blesses and encourages you to continue to go after the relationship you want to have.

— Benjamin

TABLE OF CONTENTS

Introduction 1

Chapter 1: Which Way? His Way or Her Way? 3

Chapter 2: The Importance of Covering Your Bases 7

Chapter 3: What's Your Appetite? 13

Chapter 4: Interest Rate 19

Chapter 5: What's Your Definition of it? 25

Chapter 6: Having Inferior Thinking 29

Chapter 7: We Must Protect our House 35

Chapter 8: What Are You Portraying? 41

Chapter 9: The Boy and Girl 47

Chapter 10: What's Really Important? 51

Chapter 11: Are You in Your Right Mind? 55

Chapter 12: "The Bed Undefiled" 59

In Conclusion 65

INTRODUCTION

If you're a person who sees the importance of having a healthy marriage, a stable home life, and raising successful kids, then Benjamin believes *Open Sesame: Unlocking the Hidden Doors Within Ourselves*, can be an incredible tool for you to use. *Open Sesame* is a book that can help couples have the healthy marriage they both desire. It's meant to be read by an individual with sections where the reader can take note of the opinion and insight of the special person in one's life. *Open Sesame* is an interactive book that will also guide its reader in and out of marital conversations that every healthy marriage must have or has had. Conversations for people who have said:

"Tell me what you need from me."

"Tell me what you want me to do."

"Help me understand why this is the way it is."

Hidden on the inside of us are our real thoughts, raw desires, and youthful goals in life. The intent of this book is to bring couples closer to one another and further away from the lies in the world. Closer as in a healthier sex life, better communication skills, and keeping the fun and youthfulness in their relationship. Further as in from the lies of the world when it comes to trusting men or women and allowing your kids to do whatever they want because of the world we live in.

People have had so many bad experiences in the relationship arena that it ha evolved into personal truths; now they don't know what to truly believe. We all need help with understanding and respecting each other's mentalities, but to respect something you must first understand it.

What *Open Sesame* brings to its readers is the Biblical truths concerning these matters. It will be a good idea to utilize the note-taking sections to talk with your spouse or spouse-to-be. *Open Sesame* was written for someone like you who is searching for answers that will encourage and help your relationship, to help you better understand yourself and those with whom you are in a relationship. I hope you enjoy my book and the journey.

1 WHICH WAY? HIS WAY OR HER WAY?

Growing up in different homes and being raised by different parents in different environments, of course we're going to have different views, beliefs, traditions, and philosophies in life. In this chapter, we will go over how we can have over 20 years of truth engrained or embedded in us, and then one day after our wedding, our truth is faced with change and our beliefs are challenged with opposition. How we handle that first encounter will affect how we handle all of the others during the course of our marriage.

Robyn and I were raised in similar homes with a mom and dad who worked and at least one sibling. I had a brother and sister, and she had one sister. We were from the same hometown, but we went to two different churches. So, from what I could see, we were pretty similar, until a cold day in December, right after the honeymoon.

I can remember it like it was yesterday...

I asked Robyn, "What are we eating for our Sunday dinner?"

She looked at me like, "Who's cooking dinner? Did your mom invite us over to dinner???"

I said, "No, she didn't invite us over. I thought you were going to cook!"

She said, "I hadn't planned on cooking. I didn't know what we were going to eat either. I thought you had something in mind to cook."

In my head I said, "B@#$& please! You better go in that kitchen and figure it out!"

Sorry for that typo. It's supposed to say, "Baby! Please!"

She looked at me and thought to herself, "This M#? $F#@$&! must done lost his d@#$ mind again."

Sorry for that typo again. That's supposed to say, "This man of my dreams must have lost his dang wallet again."

But back to the story, this was our first encounter with the different traditions embedded in us. I was expecting Robyn to cook me a Sunday dinner that would cover the whole table like my grandma did for my granddaddy, my aunties did for my uncles, and her mom did for her dad. But looking back at my life now, that's not what they did: they only did that for holidays, not just for the men in their lives. But anyway, back to what I was expecting Robyn to do. I was expecting a spread of food after church. Robyn wasn't expecting anything other than coming home and changing clothes.

DIFFERENT MENTALITIES

Growing up, I was the middle child but the oldest son, so I was expected to do more around the house to help out. Robyn was the baby girl and Daddy's girl, so she was not expected to help out as much around the house. I was raised to believe, **"If anyone will not work, neither shall he eat."** (2 Thessalonians 3:10). Robyn was raised to believe, **"Whatever you ask the Father in my name, will be given to you."** (John 14:13). I was raised with a "workers" mentality, and she was raised with a "ask for what you won't" mentality. I had my way of thinking and believing, and she had hers.

Even though we discussed the plans for our future with each other while dating, we didn't encounter a lot of stuff until we got married. Both of our ways were biblical, and both of our ways had worked our entire lives. So, we each believed our way was correct, but now that we were married our ways were being challenged which had us thinking: Whose way was right the right way? Somebody had to be right. There had to be a winner and a loser. A right way and a wrong way. I thought to myself: No one counts ties.

I'm sure you may have encountered similar situations where something has always worked for you, and now there's opposition against what has worked before. Having a leader mentality I was used to being right or at least use to figuring out a better way to be right. My way has worked for me for the last twenty years.

You may not be as corny as me and Robyn, but I'm sure you've experienced something similar ¬when something or someone challenges your way of doing things-such as your work ethics, cleaning ethics, or your wardrobe. The fix to this, I believe, is for you two to hear each other out with an open mind of "I might be wrong" then put your thoughts together to come up with a reasonable plan of action. We're both maybe right to an extent but not completely right. I believe once we acknowledge our differences and realize that neither one of us is completely right, we will join in agreement and work to put our ideas together. We will take what we know and match it with what our spouse knows make it work and come up with a newer way that is better for our household.

ASSIGNMENT TIME

Talk about what maybe is getting in the way of what you're trying to do accomplish in life. Come up with a solution to change it.

2
THE IMPORTANCE OF COVERING YOUR BASES

Covering your bases in marriage can be compared to housekeeping rules. One person does this; the other person does that. Each person has their own set of responsibilities even if they're shared responsibilities. Each person has to make sure they keep up their end of the deal. But sometimes in marriage, it's easy for certain responsibilities to be swept under the rug of life and overlooked. With kids, work, family, and friends it is easy for us to lay aside our responsibilities and forget about how important it is for us to keep our bases covered. In most cases, it is easier for the multi-talented person in the relationship to cover their bases of responsibilities. The importance of each person covering his or her own bases is critical to the relationship. Because you're a leader, it's easy for you to see what I am saying; but the downfall of being a leader is that, because you're used to winning, it's hard for you to accept a slacker on your team. And because you like momentum and things flowing in the right direction, it frustrates you to have to stop and check on the one that is slowing down progress.

Do you agree? (Circle one)
- Yes
- No
- Maybe so?

Your answer

Explain why you agree or disagree and why it doesn't it bother you:

_____
_____
_____
_____

Your Mate's Answer

Explain why you agree or disagree, and why it doesn't it bother you!

_____
_____
_____
_____

Not Perfect, But Better

With our bases covered, we have a higher chance to win in life. We should have a happier marriage and well-rounded kids. With all our bases covered, things just run more smoothly. The sex is great because no one is lacking in the love area. The communication is good because everyone knows what's going on since everyone is in place right where they are supposed to be. And if anyone needs help, it won't be hard to help them because we're on the same page.

Now let's see what it looks like when bases aren't covered. And since we're adults and married or going to be married, let's begin with sex. You will see throughout this book that sex is a hot topic, and the reason being is because it's all around us and we need it. And if you don't, your partner in life probably does. After God, sex between husband and wife can be the glue that keeps it together as you're both moving and grooving through life. If you don't think so, let that base be uncovered and see how things quickly fall apart or become unstable. A man and woman coming together as one is a beautiful thing.

Do you agree_____?

Does your spouse agree _____?

> Disclaimer- I am not talking about people who can't physically have sex because of health issues. I am talking about people who choose not to because they don't want to.

Talk over your answers with each other. Time and date it for your records if it had a positive response. If it did not, keep reading and we'll get behind that hidden door as we go. Stay encouraged.

Open Sesame

Let's talk about kids, if you have any. Both parents have to be on the same playing field when it comes to children because kids can be really tricky, manipulating, and aggravating — I mean loving and caring and give you a sense of fulfillment. And that's why you have to protect them, discipline them, and teach them right from wrong. The world is teaching them enough wrong as it is. So, covering the base of parenthood is important. It gives both parents the freedom to express their views on how they believe they expect their kids to be raised and a plan of action that will help those plans come alive. And because there's no one size fits all plan on how to raise children, parents have to be on the same sheet of music and not against one another when it comes to rearing their kids. Our children are little versions of ourselves. My wife and I call them little amplified versions of ourselves. What we needed when we were small, they need when they are small. What we didn't need but got when we were small, they don't need when they are small.

It can be hard at times because in the boyfriend/girlfriend stage you both are looking forward to the future, and at that stage it's easy to be like, "Yeah, I think we will have good kids together." Those are the easy days.

I'm talking about *after* you have the kids, as they're growing up. Little parts of your personality and your spouse's personality start popping out of your kids, and now you're thinking, "What are we going to do with this?" She or he is just bad and dumb. You may not think like this, but Robyn and I have. How about this: one of you is completely blind to certain things your kids do, and you don't even know it. Lil' Johnny or Lil' Jill can do no wrong in your eyes, but everyone around you is like, "Don't you think you should get them down off that chandelier?" Your little baby could be up there just a-singing and swinging that on chandelier, and all you can see is how talented he or she is. That is a sign that your parenthood base is not covered as it should be.

This base has to be covered by both parents because even if it's not driving you crazy, there's a high chance it's driving your spouse crazy. And that can cause your child to become a wedge between two good parents. That will affect the parent's communication because neither one is willing to listen to the other, which will, in turn, affect their intimacy and their prayer life. Ultimately the sex life suffers because they really can't stand one another since they're not seeing eye to eye on seemingly obvious situations. If this was happening to anyone else, you would know what they would need to do and why, but because it's your child, you think they're exempt from the consequences of their actions. One parent may say, "But it's my baby, they can't be doing such and such," while the other parent is saying, "Yes it's my baby, that's why they can do such and such!!!!" And that's why we must handle this correctly.

Parenting can be hard. As a matter of fact, it is hard. God has given you a responsibility to raise His child to a place where you can and will pass them along to Him. Understand that they may and will veer, but God's got them. Our responsibility is to do what we're supposed to do with a sober mind and raise them in a way that is pleasing to Him.

Things to Ask Yourself…
- Would God be pleased if my kid is singing and swinging from the chandelier?

- Is God pleased if my kid can justify talking back to their teacher?
- Is it pleasing to God for my kid to go to a party, listen to any kind of music, or start dating at this age?
- Is it pleasing to God for them to be doing *blank*, just because everyone else is and it seems OK?

If any of those answers are no, those are the areas you have to work on and pray about. You must do both. Pray and work on your parenting.

Real quick with the sex base being covered. You both have to learn how to fulfill each other's sexual appetite. Times are changing rapidly. Life is changing, people are changing, your kids are changing, and therefore you have to change too. You don't have to change into the ways of the world, but you may have to be able to change in a certain area. Not in a bad way, more like a phone or computer getting updated kind of way. You'll stay the same, you'll just be smarter. And believe me, your spouse will be happy. But we'll talk more about this in the next chapter, about what your spouse really needs and why and how you're the only person that can and should give it to them.

— Be ready to be updated.

3 WHAT'S YOUR APPETITE?

What do you have an appetite for? Are you willing to be honest with your spouse or spouse-to-be about your appetite? Can you tell them what you don't have an appetite for? The appetite I am referring to is for sex, affection, touching, talking, friends, foods, social media, X-rated videos, music, and success in life such as money, business, jobs, and family. These 14 needs are vital to some people. Yes, there's different strokes for different folks, but if one person has a lower appetite in at least five, the relationship may struggle in some way.

One example of having different appetites would be a man wanting to wait to have kids while his wife is ready, or vice versa. You may have a man that is gung-ho on having kids, but his wife would rather wait until later. Can you see how problems may arise? You can have a man who wants, loves, and needs sex, but his wife may rather do it once a week or every other week or, worse, once a month. Whereas the man probably would like to have it all the time, or vice versa. One may have an appetite to go shopping regularly, and the other may be like me and would rather go shopping once or twice a year. Who knows? This list can go on and on. The point is are you willing to expose your appetite to your spouse or spouse-to-be? Are you willing to expose yourself to them about your honest and real desires and wants? Have you been honest with them thus far? Can you handle them telling you what their appetites are? Or will you keep your appetites hidden from them? Often, hidden in the back of most people's minds and hearts are wants and needs that can be embarrassing to some degree. But we can't allow that to be an excuse for keeping our appetites to ourselves and hidden from the ones that can satisfy our needs.

Here's a little story about me and one of my appetites. It all started in the 3rd grade when a group of boys called me over to take a look at their magazines. So, lo and behold I looked, and it was a magazine full of naked women. It went from naked women posing to naked women kissing, then to naked women doing everything under the sun. As a 9- or 10-year-old little boy, my flesh was being fed by naked images that I wasn't looking for at the beginning. Someone else started this in me. They gave me an appetite for sex and sexual images. From 10-12 it grew, climaxing at 13. I began to watch videos. By the age of 16-18, I began looking for girls to have sex with. By 19, I was experiencing it. Now I'm pushing 40 and still struggling with images and a strong sexual appetite.

My appetite caused tension in my marriage. The worst thing my wife had ever seen when I married her was the "so-called" sex scene on her channel 4 soap opera. That's it. So, when you weigh each of our experiences against each other, I beat her in the 3rd grade. Can you see how different our expectations were? Can you see how awkward some of our conversations had to have been? Can you see how embarrassing it was for both of us? Robyn had a man that enjoyed pornography. I looked like a sinner in her eyes. And I had a "Miss Goody Two Shoes" as a wife. Granted, that was one of the first things that attracted each of us to the other: my smooth and cool ways and her stand-out-from-the-crowd personality. But behind my slick ways was a guy who had hidden expectations from his wife.

THE DILEMMA

Just like food for our bodies, our appetites have fed our character, making us become the men and women we are today. There are parts of us that have been fed by things our spouses knew nothing about, and because of our appetite which created the very thing that attracted them to us. This puts us in a dilemma mentality. Getting married, becoming a Christian, eating healthy, and budgeting all puts us on a better path. The dilemma is once we're married, we're not supposed to look at inappropriate and X-rated material. Being a Christian, we're not supposed to be willing to do anything wrong. Eating healthy meant no more going out to our favorite restaurants. Budgeting means we can't do anything we used to call fun. We took away everything we liked and became bored and boring. So, what do you do?

Personally, we may feel that our personality is changing and becoming unattractive to our spouses. We feel if we were able to feed our appetite like we used to that we'd feel better about ourselves and still be attractive to our spouse. What do we do when our present life needs a little bit of past life to help us, as a couple, make it to our future?

People are getting divorced left and right because they can't answer questions in this book. In my opinion, I need to learn new stuff to keep things going in my life because that's how Robyn and I started off: fun, new and adventurous. I believe we shouldn't lose that fun part of ourselves just because we're parents, spouses, and Christians.

A Bible verse that I stand strongly on is Ecclesiastes 7:16-18 which reads, **"So don't be too good or too wise! Why destroy yourself? On the other hand, don't be too wicked either. Don't be a fool! Why die before your time? Pay attention to these instructions, for anyone who fears God will avoid both extremes."**

This scripture freed me to be me. I don't believe we should ever lose who we are to a certain degree. What do you and your spouse believe when it comes to keeping your appetites fed and under control? _____

_____
_____
_____
_____
_____
_____

I believe you have to be a mature adult to share it. I believe you have to be even stronger to listen and meet the needs of your spouse. Be smart, be understanding, and be clear on what's good for you and what's not. I believe you know.

Open Sesame

4 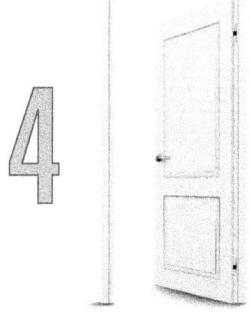 INTEREST RATE

In this chapter we will be talking about the ways to keep your interest rate up and the reasons why it's important in your marriage for the longevity of the relationship. Have you ever heard anyone say, "I'm not interested in you anymore," "I'm not interested in them anymore," or "I'm just not interested in that anymore," and wondered what could have happened for them to get to that point or what could have been done differently to avoid that from happening?

Keeping the interest rate up in a relationship is vital to the longevity of any relationship. It's one of the most important hinges next to trust, honesty, love, faithfulness, sex, and faith in God. Your interest in your spouse or spouse-to-be is one of the first attractions you had for them and they had for you. Its importance

is not really spoken much about but leads the way to the other attractions in a relationship. The seven attractions in relationships are usually:
1. Interest
2. Trust
3. Love
4. Honesty
5. Faithfulness
6. Sex
7. Faith in God

First, we have to be interested in someone. Then we have to be sure we can trust them before we love them. They have to be honest with us for us to believe they will be faithful to us. The sex has to be good with the potential of getting better, and if they love God that's a bonus and a must. I know that this doesn't sound biblically correct, and I'm not encouraging single people to have sex, but I believe for most couples, this is the order they followed when they found their mate. **{This saying is for all of us who jumped the gun and didn't wait until marriage to have sex.}** If neither person had to persuade the other to follow Christ, everything else in the relationship will follow suit, if and only if you keep the interest rate up. If you don't keep the interest rate up, it doesn't matter how much they love the Lord, how good the sex is, or how faithful, honest, loving, and trustworthy they are: Nothing else would matter if either of us lose interest. Interest is one of the things that turned your eye toward your mate.

Remember, what it took to get them is what it's going to take to keep them. We will all change over time, and times will change, so we both have to be willing to change for the health of our relationship. We can stay the same fun-loving people we are, but we have to be willing to adapt to one another as our needs change. Look at it like updating your phone. You can update yourself with new information. Try going to different places, eat different foods, learn a new dance, learn a new sex move, just do something new together or for each other.

It's really not that hard to do to keep things interesting between you two. It's important to do something because if you don't, just like an outdated phone, you won't seem to be any good to the person you're with. Or a better way of saying it is that you won't be as up to date as you can be for them. You're still the person they fell in love with—you may just need some updating so that the interest rate won't drop in your relationship.

When reading this book, you may have found yourself with low interest or a loss of interest in your spouse. My prayer for you is that you regain that interest by being honest with yourself and your spouse on why you lost it and be willing to work on those areas. Losing interest in someone or something can be embarrassing, intimidating, and discouraging to another person, so deal with it cautiously. Deal with this matter lovingly and with a mission. It can also be relaxing, refreshing, and renewing to a couple's relationship, so deal with it intentionally.

As believers and leaders in whatever areas we lead in, working on our interest is important because those whom we are leading are watching us as an example of what a couple should be. People closest to us can usually sense when we're not interested in something important. They may not say anything, but they can tell something's up. Our leadership is important, so don't let anything discourage you or make you want to give up.

If you're a fresh couple, my prayer for you is that you start early on keeping your interest up. Continue to do what you're doing now and stay in that lane of fresh happiness. Don't allow life to bump you into the slow lane or bump you onto an exit route you're not supposed to take and take you on a detour that wasn't meant for you.

Assignment #1
- Talk about the things in your life that you're interested in now: good or bad. Why? Because if it's good or bad, it still has your attention, so your mate needs to know. You both need to talk about it, so you'll know what to work on or pray about. The Bible says, **"For where your treasure is, there your heart will be also."** (Matt. 6:21 NIV)

So, whether they know or not, your mind, heart, and interest will end up being there anyway. Give them the dignity of knowing where you are and where you may not be wanting to go. Write "complete" when you're finished:

_____
_____
_____

Assignment #2
- Talk and write down areas where you want your interest to be raised. Things you want changed, things you want to stop or start. New things you've noticed on the internet that you like. Things on the internet you may be addicted to or just like watching or playing:

_____
_____
_____

Assignment #3
- Write down what you think can help your marriage now that wouldn't have worked in the past:

_____
_____
_____

Assignment #4
- Write down what can make you happy now:

_____
_____
_____

Assignment #5
- Tell each other, "We can do better, and I promise to make things better."

I know some people don't make promises, so use your own word for saying you're committed to making things better between you two even if everything is good now. It's always good to hear this from one another for assurance.

5 WHAT'S YOUR DEFINITION OF IT?

Everyone has their own opinions when it comes to events such as politics, religion, education, and so on. What I want to bring to our attention is the definition you and I already have in mind for certain words: words such as *love, honor, respect, loyalty, and submission*. Believe it or not, we all have our own personal definition to words like these, and how we define them will affect the flow of conversations we have. Our definitions have more weight to them than our opinions. A definition is a truth we believe in, an opinion is how we see something at face value. A definition has been understood for a long time. Words that were defined to us years ago either by a parent, friend, or some kind of life experience. Our definition to words has a heavy presence in our belief system. We can avoid many disagreements and misunderstandings once we realize when to ask our mates, "What's your definition of it?"

Webster's Dictionary can say one thing, you or your spouse could say another, and the Bible may say yet another. For example, the Bible defines *love* as: patient and kind; not jealous or boastful or proud or rude. It does not demand its own way. It is not irritable, and it keeps no record of being wronged. It does not rejoice about injustice but rejoices whenever the truth wins out. Love never gives up, never loses faith, is always hopeful, and endures through every circumstance.

Webster's Dictionary defines love as an intense feeling of deep affection and a great pleasure and interest in something. And I define love as giving up your own selfish ambitions for someone else to be happy before you are. Define what *love* means to you:

_____
_____
_____

Let's pick another word like *submission*. Submission is a very unpopular word these days. No one wants to be known as the person who has to submit. Everyone wants to be the Boss. But the Bible is very clear on how it should be used and when and where it should be used. I believe when people say submission, everyone hears their own definition of it. How would you define submission? _____
_____

We can use words such as respect, *loyalty*, and almost any other word, and I believe we all have our own definitions for them. And if we all have our own definition of common words, we can easily misunderstand what someone else is saying. Can you see how easy it is for someone misunderstand you?

A word like *marriage* may not be misunderstood, but with marriage comes words like *love, submission, loyalty, sex,* and *respect.*

How we define our own words will dictate the direction of our conversation. And if we don't know how to learn each other's definitions of words, we will be in a constant misunderstanding and frustrated state of communication. Think back to your last disagreement or misunderstanding. Do you think the definition of something that was said could have been the problem all along? And that's why they couldn't see things your way? Fascinating isn't it?

My wife and I used to have a horrible time talking to one another, trying to get each other to understand what we were talking about. After we learned how to recognize the differences in our definitions, we easily fixed our communication problem. All we had to do was ask, "What's your definition of it?"

I believe once this is learned in a relationship, communicating will be much easier. It may not be a quick fix, but it will remove tension, and when the tension is removed, things will loosen up where it will be easier to work on things.

Open Sesame

6 HAVING INFERIOR THINKING

No one wants to be inferior. No one wants to feel inferior. No one should be made to feel inferior. Inferiority comes from doubt, disbelief, and fear. Inferiority is being lower in rank, status, quality, or position than someone else. In this chapter, we will discuss how to help and understand someone with inferior thinking, mainly when it affects you or someone else when they haven't done anything wrong to trigger an inferior way of thinking.

Inferior thinking comes from past events. It's the fear of something going wrong now because of what happened in the past. It's the fear of a past event repeating itself.

The best way I've learned to deal with inferior thinking is to talk out my fears of what might happen to either my wife or

> The best way I've learned to deal with inferior thinking is to talk out my fears of what might happen to either my wife or a good guy friend. Try your best to not share personal fears with the opposite sex because it creates a hidden bond of trust between the two of you that will be hard to break, which will complicate things in your marital relationship. Believe me— ¬been there, done that, bought that t-shirt.

a good guy friend. Try your best to not share personal fears with the opposite sex because it creates a hidden bond of trust between the two of you that will be hard to break, which will complicate things in your marital relationship. Believe me— ¬been there, done that, bought that t-shirt.

The only reason I was having inferior thoughts is because of what I believed I was seeing. Once I'm allowed to talk out my thoughts, I can first release my fear of what I'm thinking and then have whoever I'm talking to explain to me what's really going on so I can see the reality. The key here is to believe the person with whom you are speaking.

For example, I'm a dad of five wonderful kids, I have a great family life—it may not be perfect, but it's a great life for me. With that being said, as a dad I have certain fears and concerns when it comes to my daughters and my son. So when I notice certain things in their personality or hear stories from school or realize what's available to them these days, it's hard for me to believe they've got it all under control and that everything is going to be fine and I have nothing to worry about. That's not the way my mind works because I tend to struggle with all that's available to me on my phone and in the world we're living in right now¬ and I'm not involved in it as much as they are. My kids go to school and are around all sorts of different types of personalities— kids that are into all the new trends and fads and who are willing to teach each other anything they may want to know. So, time and time again, my wife and I have conversations about how we see life and what we think we should do about it.

Life isn't easy for anyone trying to live the straight and narrow life. There's a lot of stuff we can feel inferior to and be inferior to. My wife has helped me get over my inferior thinking because, yes, there's a lot that can go wrong. But talking it out and praying about it does help. You may not be a believer, but I pray that you become one because I don't believe we can live a happy life without faith.

The Bible says in Psalm 121:2 in the NKJV, **"My help comes from the Lord, Who made heaven and earth."**

When dealing with inferior thinking when it comes to our present, past, or future, we need to talk about it and pray about it. No medicine can cure inferior thinking.

There are so many different communities of people in this social media-infested world *typing* about life and what's going on with them, but never *talking* about it. We take pictures and share videos, but never share what's really important to us. Inferior thinking can block God's blessing in our lives because it stops us from moving forward and being set free due to fear. I recommend talking to someone no matter how severe or how small your inferior thinking may be. If you're strong and have no problems with this, help someone else see things the way you do. ONLY IF ITS A GODLY POINT OF VIEW.

Here are signs of inferior thinking:
1. Thinking your mate is going to leave you for someone else.
2. Believing your spouse's ex is better than you.
3. Believing your spouse will cheat on you.
4. Comparing yourself to your spouse's ex on more than one level.
5. Believing you will never be enough for your spouse.

Side Effects of Inferior Thinking:
1. Positive one minute, the world is falling apart the next minute.
2. Nice and loving one minute, snappy with an attitude the next minute.
3. Always worried about the future of your relationships.
4. Making unnecessary remarks about each other and the relationship.

Ways to correct inferior thinking:
1. Talk about it. Be willing to share how you really feel about a situation.
2. Be willing to listen and believe what the person with whom you're speaking has to say.
3. Stop doubting what those close to you are saying.
4. Start believing something positive about yourself.
5. Begin to pray: Ask God for help in your particular situation.
6. Stop doubting. Start believing.

Open Sesame

7 WE MUST PROTECT OUR HOUSE

The reason for protecting our house is simple. We have an enemy who wants to steal, kill and destroy everything we have. He wants to steal our offspring and everything we produce. He wants to kill our relationships and our influence. He wants to destroy our identity and the purpose God has given us. Not just ours but also our kids' and our grandkids': He wants the legacy and lineage God has given us.

Protecting one's house is every homeowner's responsibility. From multiple door locks and alarm systems to security cameras, security fences, guard dogs, and neighborhood watchers, homeowners take protecting their homes seriously because it's not just a home; its what's inside the house that matters most. The same mindset should be taken with regard to our marriages.

We should have multiple keys to lock and unlock the doors that give access to our lives. We should have an alarm system in place that will alert us when a burglary is occurring. We should have security cameras watching over each other and our kids. We should have boundaries set up like a fence where we allow people to see our front yard but not our backyard without permission. We should have guard dogs and neighborhood watchers as friends who are committed to watching over us and being there for us to talk to if they see anything suspicious going on around us that we may not be seeing ourselves.

As married couples, we should take our home life seriously. We must be committed to protecting our homes, whether it's kids and their future, our marriage and our future, or our lives in general. Protecting our homes is for the present and the future—present because we must be on guard right now; future because what we're doing right now will affect what happens later.

Seeing the importance of protecting your home will give both longevity and good health. You will create prosperity for your family because everyone will be able to take care of themselves, and you will hopefully give your kids a Biblical foundation for their lives, along with education and good ethics.

I believe as believers and leaders we are to make sure we are feeding ourselves daily with positive messages and music to keep us in the right frame of mind and under a godly influence. A little bit of secular music is good for us too, I believe. It keeps us hip. In my opinion, it's necessary for us to know what our children are listening to in order for us to better cover all our bases when it comes to protecting our house. Every now and then tune in to their favorite radio station on your way to or from school to see what the popular songs are. Sometimes I'll pull off one of their ear buds or ear pods to listen to what they're listening to while they're doing their homework. If they're listening to something you prefer they not listen to, tell them not to or at least not listen to it at home; in doing this you set boundaries for your house, and allowing them to see that they can't just do anything in your home.

Other ways of protecting our house include going to church and being involved in church. This teaches our kids that there's something bigger than us and our family that we must serve and delegate our time to.

I believe that going on dates and setting aside quality time for each other will also help with protecting our home. By us getting away and making sure we are okay as a couple, we'll know what frame of mind each of us have and what obstacles we both may be facing through our week. Setting aside time for each other is critical for our relationship because in doing so we're making sure no one is handling anything alone when we may need some help or someone to talk to.

There are so many activities that can get us off our bases. Working *too* much, being *too* involved in church, family, and kids' after-school events are some examples. Being *too* involved in these areas or similar areas can weaken the strength of our home protection because we're spreading ourselves *too* thin. Yes, a lot of activities can be good but there is a saying— ¬too much of anything isn't good for us.

Learning how to choose our family's activities before any seasons begin takes strategic planning so that no last-minute decisions will be made. This helps because there is no place for chaos when making a decision due to pressure of time.

Strategic planning should happen even for positive events like church, after-school activities, and little Johnny's and little Jill's performances. Let's be honest with ourselves and our spouses and admit that we don't like to see our spouses have to go through the process of getting everything ready to go to practice or having to go through the headache ourselves of being in traffic along with other frustrated, overwhelmed parents. Yes, we see the better behavior and improvement in our kids as a result of all the practices, I hope; but from personal experience, all these activities can elevate friction at home. At times it is because we already finished a hard day at work and truly just want to slow things down for a moment and relax and spend time with our spouse without having to set time aside to do so. Because sometimes we secretly wish our spouses would go out of their way to do something for us with the same determination and dedication that they give to everyone else.

If we give a fraction of the effort that we give others to our spouses I believe our home lives will flourish into great marriages.

- How do you believe your home life will flourish?_____

Our problem is that because we're so wrapped up in the fast pace of life, we can't get a word in to say what's our problem. We're all in too big of a rush to listen to each other and see what's really going on.

I applaud you for reading this book and slowing down for a moment. While I have your attention, I want you to check the environment of your house to make sure everything is secure and protected. Check on your kids, check on your spouse, and check to see if anything needs to be repaired in your house. In doing so you are making sure your house is intact internally.

Now let's look at social media and see how we can protect our house from the outside in. I say "outside in" because it's information from the outside coming into your house through a device. In my opinion, social media has become the #1 killer of marriages and meaningful relationships right now if you ask me. It's one of those double-edged sword kind of topic. It's good on one hand and bad on the other. You must be really mature to have a thriving marriage and a respectful social site. There are a lot of people who are very dependent and attached to social media. Some are blinded to reality; some are straight up against it; some are not affected by it at all. What I want to happen now is for you and your spouse to talk this over and come up with a plan and an agreement on what is the best way to protect your marriage from the #1 killer, social media. Do it respectfully. Do all you can do to protect your house for your family. It's not always easy but it's needed to win. You can do it.

8 WHAT ARE YOU PORTRAYING?

Do you know anyone whose personality changes when they get around other people, but the weird thing is that they don't know it? Have you ever experienced this? An example of this is how a man may act around a very beautiful woman or how a woman may act around a very handsome man. They're obviously attracted to them, but they're trying to keep their cool so no one will notice it. Another example is how someone may act when they're around people of authority such as a pastor, police, or their boss. They stumble over their words or try to avoid them altogether.

I believe this comes from the little boy or girl hidden in us that comes out every now and then. But I will to talk about that later in the book. What I want to talk about now is how we are growing and changing. There are parts of us that are still growing but not totally grown. Still in the process of changing but not finished. We're adults but not grownups like our parents. Almost there but haven't crossed the finish line.

As married couples, churchgoers, business owners, employees, or single people we are all in a process of a positive lifestyle change and are constantly trying to live up to a better standard of life. We're not quite there, but we're trying. But through trying, we may fail because life's situations can sometimes be new to us.

Hidden in our subconscious is our past—the old us, our old ways, the way we used to act or feel around other people. And since this can be hidden in our subconscious mind, we tend to react without even thinking. Sometimes we have no clue that we may have just turn into "that ol' playa of a man," coward, or "Loudmouth sweet 16-year-old hair-twirling girl" that we might have once been.

Some people turn up by acting extra. Some people turn down by shying down and becoming invisible. *Why is all this important, Ben?* You may be asking. Because first of all, you don't even know that you change around people you shouldn't be changing around. And second, your mate is watching you do this, and they are in shock like, *what is this such and such doing?*

When we change, we portray something we're not. When we change, those around us who know us see us being someone we're not. And the question is, Why? Why do we or they feel that we have to change? What makes other people so important that it alters someone else's character? And on the flip side of that thought, does the person who changes know how they're changing? And if they think they do, are they changing into what they are trying to portray, because a lot of times people don't. But they think they are.

Here are some examples. You're new on a job, and you want to give your best effort, but in doing so you give a little extra and look like a kiss-up. Or you're new to a neighborhood, church, school, or something along those lines, and you're checking out the scene, but you actually look like a judge, spectator, and critic. Or on the flip side of that, you can be the other person who is meeting the neighbor, church member, or student, and you look like the judge, spectator, or critic. No matter which one you may be or what you portray when you meet new people, they are going to take that first impression to heart. So, you have to be careful about how you act for the sake of your mate. Keep in mind the goal here is to keep the comfort level between you two peaceful while you both go through new, tough terrains in life together.

Let's think about the family side of portraying. For instance, you may have a blended family. In the past, you've been able to avoid a lot of time with your ex because of work or living in another state, but now you must spend time with your ex because your kids want to meet their family. So now you and your ex must bite the bullet and spend time with each other's family if you haven't already been doing it. What do you do now? How do you stay calm and collected around your ex and your spouse? How do you keep the peace while facing a mistake? Your child is not a mistake, but *you* made a mistake a long time ago, and now you have to face the reality of your past in your present. That may sound harsh to say, but it's real for some people, and they don't know how to handle this moment that can make or break good families if not handled correctly and respectfully.

Without a plan of understanding, this can make your present relationship awkward. In most situations where a relationship ends on an awkward note——such as two people who really had other plans for their relationship getting together, having sex, and making a baby—the former couple and their new spouses wish they hadn't gotten together and made a baby. For most couples in this situation, they would rather the relationship had ended, and they had gone their separate ways, but now the parents have to deal with it and everything that comes along with it, such as birthdays, holidays, and family events. The question is, how do we deal with this and keep peace amongst everyone?

Whether we are portraying to be this or that, what we portray in the moment can be critical to those who know us best. The goal in this chapter is for us to be able to confront one another in love and say, "Hey I don't like it when you change when your around them. I don't think it's necessary and it makes me uncomfortable because I'm not used to you acting like that." And your spouse may say, "Where did that come from? How did you get to that conclusion?" Because, most people don't voice their opinions about this kind of stuff. We voice our opinion about a lot of other stuff but not this.

I once heard in a church service from a pastor about how he had to change what he portrayed because, in the pulpit, he was a happy man of faith who loved to talk at church, but at home he would keep to himself and not talk to his kids or his wife. Years later, his kids came to him and told him how they felt. So, he decided to change, because hidden in the back of his mind, that's how he believed things were supposed to go. The problem was he gave all his good energy to the church and had nothing to give to his family. This portrayed a man who loved and cared about other people more than his family. Yet he did love and care about his own family; he just portrayed something else, and what he portrayed took a toll on his family. This happens all the time in different scenarios. The problem is how it affects other people. It takes courage to confront a person who can't see how they're behaving when they think they're doing something else.

We've all done it. We just didn't know it at the time and how often we did it. And in that way, it's done without the sensitivity of a spouse's views, feelings, and thoughts that can give us an understanding. The atmosphere in our house may become and stay awkward if we're not aware of it. Especially when we look our happiest when we're with someone else or doing something else. What we portray matters. We have to recognize this and begin to catch ourselves.

BLENDED FAMILY QUESTION

The parent of your child has to come around because of the child. Your better half has to endure this because of you or vice versa, because of them. How do you two stay on one accord with all of this? Are you both mature enough to not let it bother you one bit, or do you keep your true feelings hidden inside and act like all is well and like everything is hunky dory?

Answer Here:
- Are you both good with the situation? Yes or No:_____
- Do you have something to work on? _____
  in your opinion. And _____
  in your mate's opinion.

How do you think you overcame this and unlocked any hidden regret, embarrassment, shame in either of you?
_____
_____

9 THE BOY AND GIRL

"**When I was a child, I spake as child, I understood as a child, I thought as a child; but when I became a man, I put away childish things.**" (1 Corinthians 13:11)

But when I became a man, I put away childish things. When I came to my senses, I knew what to do. When I stopped thinking childishly, I knew what to say. Once I understood who I was, I knew what to put away. This is what I call the transitional moment of life: when a child becomes an adult.

But, what do you do when you find someone still struggling with childish things in their mid-20s, early 30s, late 40s, or even 50s? Still struggling with lying, cheating, irresponsibility, or selfishness? What makes someone want to stay like this? I don't know! That's why I am asking you. What I'm here to talk about in this chapter is what to do with the boy or girl in us that keeps getting us into trouble or has the potential to get us in trouble and prevents us from living the life we really want.

There have been times in my life when right before something good was about to happen in my life, something in me would either hesitate in moving forward, rebel against what I knew to be true, or just give in to some sinful act, which caused the good thing I was expecting to just pass right by me, leaving me empty-handed and disappointed. There have also been times in my life when I wanted to be faithful and holy by not looking at inappropriate videos, times when I told myself I wouldn't cuss this person out for pulling their car out in front of me or speak to a woman that was looking my way with a smile on her face. Moments when I would think:

"I want to do what is good, but I don't. I don't want to do what is wrong, but I do it anyway." (Romans 7: 19 NLT)

There are lots of times when something in me just wanted what it wanted so badly in spite of the consequences and went after it, hoping no one would know or find out what I did. Kind of childish, you think?

Sound familiar? Hopefully not, it's probably just me. But what I've learned about myself is this: whenever I have those spurts of selfishness or moments of carelessness, I've allowed the boy in me to come out and take the lead in my decision making. I've allowed this immature state of thinking to override my mature and logical way of thinking. Following bad decision after bad decision, failure after failure, mistake after mistake, I had to learn how to get a grip on "this boy" in me and be set free from him by putting away those childish things.

But first I had to realize what childish ways I had and what things I had to put away and why.
- Childish speaking
- Childish understanding
- Childish thinking

These three actions are the most visible actions that can hinder us from growing up: the way we speak to ourselves and others, the way we perceive life and timing, and with what and whom we entertain our time all dictate our maturity.

List three (3) things that you can put away right now to speed up the process of becoming the person you know you can be:

1. _____
2. _____
3. _____

Some examples are:
- Excessive social media time
- Gaming time, screen time, internet usage
- Excessive ap, Rock, Country, music time
- Friends of bad influence, drugs, alcohol
- Excessive fast food and processed foods

Now list four (4) things you can add to your life that can enhance your life:

1. _____
2. _____
3. _____
4. _____

Some examples are:
- Reading
- Any form of exercise
- Listening to a positive, educational, inspirational message and more gospel music
- Goal setting

With these seven actions, you can change your life. Maybe not overnight, but over a determined length of time and mindset it can be done. Discuss your answers together and come up with a plan to change into the man or woman you are destined to be.

10 WHAT'S REALLY IMPORTANT?

Winning, Losing, Forfeiting, Quitting, or Cheating

We've all heard the following sayings: "Cheaters never win." "Never give up, never ever give up." "Don't throw in the towel." "Do whatever it takes to win." "You better stop while you're ahead."

All these sayings came from moments of adversity, at a time when something was on the line in athletics, an occupation, a dream, or a marriage.

In this chapter, we will examine when it is the best time to fight and when it is the best time to take flight. How not to major on the minors or minor on the majors. How to not take certain situations too seriously, and how not to take certain situations too lightly. Most people know the answers to those statements when they're not in adverse moments. But what I've noticed is that

In the moment of confrontation, we tend to forget what's really important, to take matters into our own hands, and do what we believe is best for us and our situation. As flawed individuals and not expert people who know everything about everything, we can easily make a mistake in judgment and jeopardize the things in our life that will cost us later.

When coming up with conclusions and making decisions for those conclusions, we have to know how to weigh out the pros and cons and the do's and don'ts and the "what we want to happen" vs. the "what we don't want to happen." Most of the time when it comes to couples, one person needs details and the other needs facts. Facts about what's going on right now and what happened. And the other may need details on what caused something to happen and why. In reality, facts and details go hand-in-hand, but because they look and seem so different it is hard for some couples to see that they are the same and agree that they go hand-in-hand. One may need to know the end-game result and the other may need to know how the process will go.

What I'm hoping for in this time together is how we can draw the line in the sand of understanding so we won't have to cross the line, and fuss and fight at crucial times that will spill over into other moments, when all we should, would, and could have done was to have recognized what's really important during the moment and stop before we entered into the area of fussing and disagreeing. Because when you're in the area of fussing and fighting, it can be like walking down a long road with no end in sight. It's common for couples to be at odds with each other and stop talking, but that's not healthy for the relationship. If you're new to marriage and haven't experienced this, take note of what I'm saying because you're already ahead of the game. But—and that's a Big ol' BUT—if you're married and *have* experienced this, let's change our technique because it is bringing division between the two of you.

Ways of changing your technique:

First, recognize what you tend to do when you are confronted with doing the right thing and making a decision you believe is right.

1. Are you the type of person that likes to win and is motivated by winning? I _____ but my spouse _____
2. Do you hate being wrong or losing? I _____ but my spouse _____
3. Would you rather just throw in the towel because you hate confrontation, and therefore just let other people win even though you're probably right?
I _____ but my spouse _____
4. Do you usually just say "the heck with it" because you don't think you would win or because you'd rather not go through the process of winning?
I _____ but my spouse _____
5. Do you usually talk fast or loudly to shout over the other person in order to dominate them so they'll quit or be confused so they'll stop just so that you can win?
I _____ but my spouse _____

Depending on your answer, you may miss what's important because you're only considering yourself and what you want and like.

In relationships, it is important to focus on what matters: the marriage, the kids, your household, the standards of God, right and wrong, moral and immoral.

We live in a world that is doing a pretty good job of changing the standard of living. What we must be aware of is not allowing the worldview to influence our view. We can't allow social sites to dictate our lives just because the world is changing. We have to acknowledge that the world is changing but not allow it to change *our* world. This can be hard because most people today are so used to following the next new trend so that it can give them something new to do. If it works for you keep doing it, but if it doesn't, stop. What's really important is that we do the right thing for us and our family, despite how badly we may want something, despite if we agree or disagree, despite if we see it or not. Focus on what's important. Winning is fun, losing is not, forfeiting is something no one likes, quitting is an easy way out, and cheating is tempting.

What I would like for you to do now is to take some time from reading and think about the thoughts you may have had while reading. Stop and write down anything you agreed with or disagreed with and talk it over with your spouse. Add any notes or comments you may have here.

_____

_____

_____

_____

_____

11 ARE YOU IN YOUR RIGHT MIND?

"*For the grace of God that brings salvation has appeared to all men, teaching us that, denying <u>ungodliness</u> and <u>worldly lusts</u>, we should live **soberly**, righteously, and godly in the present age..." Titus 2:11-12 (NKJV)*

We all should be sober-minded, meaning we shouldn't let what we see, hear and experience on a day-to-day bases influence the way we think, how we make decisions, and how we view people. All the bad that can be seen and heard these days can influence our thinking by clouding our minds with lust, hate, and fear if we allow it to. With social media leading the way, we as believers and leaders must equip our minds to stay sober. The Bible says in 1 Peter 4:7 (NKJV):

"But the end of all things is at hand; therefore, <u>be serious and watchful in your prayers.</u>"

This lets us know we must stay alert because of the times we are living in and the things that are going on around us. My wife scrolls past all the beautiful women on social media and fear tries to cloud her view because she's thinking, "Oh my God, they're just letting it all hang out." I can see the exact same thing and lust clouds my thinking. Someone may see a news update and hate clouds their thinking. Someone else may see the exact same news report and fear hits them.

Being sober-minded and staying in our right state of mind is a benefit to us and those connected to us because it keeps us grounded in our thinking and not under the influence of anything else.

The Bible says in 1 Peter 5:8 (NKJV), **"Be sober, be vigilant; because your adversary the devil walks about like a roaring lion, seeking whom he may devour."**

Having a clear conscience and a correct perspective on life keeps you safe. Staying away from or limiting your time on social media sites and excessive news time can help keep your mind sober, in my opinion. A major key in staying sober-minded is knowing when you're not in your right frame of mind. My wife and I call it "being off." Social media, the news, gossiping friends and family members can all throw us "off," and that will affect the way we see things and the decisions that we make.

What do I mean when I say, "being off?" I mean not seeing things correctly; having a bad judgment; being a couple steps behind; or reading from a different sheet of music. When we're "off," we miss things like our kids' bad attitudes and we let them get away with it. When we're off, we can run a red light or stop sign. When we're off, we can have conversations with each other and not remember what we talked about 10 minutes ago, which can cause a problem later in the day when we don't do what we agreed on earlier. When people are off, they make bad decisions at the worst times. When we are off, everything looks OK, but something in the atmosphere is different. When we're off we forget important stuff. We do things we wouldn't normally do and say things we wouldn't normally say. But when we're "sober" we make all the right decisions, we catch the little things our kids do, we know what our spouse is doing and why, we know when something is wrong, and we deal with it head on. Being off causes major problems, and the scary thing about it is everything looks fine. Being off is so subtle that it's barely seen until something bad happens—passing a stop sign, saying yes when you would normally say no, not being there for someone when you normally would be.

The best way to fix this is not by fussing and not by leaving but by talking, saying "Hey did you notice what happened today? Do you remember what you said to me earlier? Can you tell that something is different between us right now? Babe, something is wrong, I think one of us is off. This is not our normal."

The main reason for this to be fixed is because our enemy loves for us to be off and against one another. The devil thrives on confusion, isolation, and division. He loves for us to accuse one another by suggesting to us in heated conversations our faults and shortcomings. This is where he usually creeps in and makes a mess of things in our relationships.

As believers and leaders, we cannot allow this to happen or else we will allow him to beat us and win. We can have all the faith and love in the world, but if we can't see where we are letting the enemy into our head and thoughts, we'll never defeat him. We can't win in life on our own.

Ecclesiastes 4:9-12 NKJV says, *"Two are better than one, Because they have a good reward for their labor. For if they fall, one will lift up his companion. But woe to him who is alone when he falls, For he has no one to help him up. Again, if two lie down together, they will keep warm; But how can one be warm alone? Though one may be overpowered by another, two can withstand him. And a threefold cord is not quickly broken."*

If you're single while reading this, it's OK. Don't be down on yourself. You have the Lord on your side, and I believe He is equipping and preparing you for you +2. There will be times in your life when you have only you to depend on, but as a couple, a leading couple, it's going to take both of you in it to win it. You both have to stay sober-minded, but when one is off alert the other and talk about it and reel each other back into reality. Then go back out and conquer your day.

— Stay Sober

12 "THE BED UNDEFILED"

"*Marriage is honorable among all, and the bed undefiled; but fornicators and adulterers God will judge.*" (Hebrews 13:4 NKJV)

Our marriages make our bed undefiled, meaning in the context of our marriage and bedroom, God sees sex as pure, clean, and holy. But what do we do when someone in the marriage sees something as unclean or a little out of their comfort zone? Let me explain. Growing up as a curious and horny teenage boy, I found ways to look up naked women. I had friends who had videos that they got from their uncles, and I had friends that had magazines, so about the time I was a man I had already seen everything under the sun when it came to sex. By the time I was married, I had already developed an appetite for sex. I had a baggage of expectations, hopes and dreams, signs and wonders for my marriage bed.

But let's talk about the woman I married. I married a "good girl," a girl that hadn't seen much or been around sex in her life. She heard stuff at school, but she didn't have those midnight TV shows like me. So, what do you do when there are two completely different views and expectations of sex in marriage? Yeah, you can say, "Ben you have the chance to show the way." Yeah, you're right. There are some things I can, but what do you do with the stuff you can't? I can't demonstrate it. Can you imagine that, me saying, "Hey, like all you got to do is grab it like this and …"? "Is you crazy? I'm not doing that. Don't even think about it." Yeah it can be said that sometimes people may just have to say what they want outright. Often, that is the most effective way to accomplish something, even in the bedroom.

But I have a problem with that. To do that regularly and consistently bothers me to the point of not doing anything or wanting anything.

Do you see this problem? We're not the only people who are like this. There are other couples who have had this same problem and not talked about it. Or at least no one I know has talked about it. But what I have heard is, "Benjamin, I'm not happy at home. She's not doing it for me anymore. I am not interested in her anymore." I've also heard women say, "I'm not interested in all that, that's too much for me."

So how do we as believers and leaders fix this gap? Usually the man does have more desires and expectations of sex than the woman, "statically speaking." I have also heard from a good friend that women are often conditioned to feel shame about their own desires and expectations, so they push them away or deny them. Unfortunately, the problem is we as couples don't necessarily talk about our true desires. We might mention it, but we don't talk deeply about it, we don't go into great detail to reveal what we may truly want. We don't talk about how we are affected when we don't get what we need. It's like a domino effect: I miss out on this, then I miss out on that, and then everything else falls apart.

We don't talk about where it might have come from. We don't talk about what we believe we can do to get over it, nor do we share what we believe will help us get over it. We miss opportunities that can make us better and draw us closer as a couple. We leave our thoughts locked up and hidden behind doors of Shame, Loneliness, Hurt, and Regret.

From a man's point of view, I understand that some men won't ask for something they desire. But after so many times if his needs aren't met, he might begin thinking or looking somewhere else to get it. Hopefully not, but most of the time he—and maybe she—does too. Most men do not like to ask a woman to satisfy him sexually, he prefers for her to already know what to do, particularly if they have been together for some length of time. But some women on the other hand prefer for her husband to tell her what to do when it comes to his sexual needs. For some men that can shut him down if he must constantly ask his wife or tell his wife what to do.

What do you think about this? Men: do you mind telling your wife what you need? Yes or No _____ And Why?_____

Open Sesame

_____
_____
_____ Ladies: Does your husband shut down _____ or is he OK with telling you what he needs? _____
_____?

Something to consider when you're trying to have and maintain a healthy sex life is each other's real needs. Not expectations, not what you were told a man wants or what a woman needs. In talking about what does Mr. _____ want and expects, and what does Mrs. _____ want and expect. Talk about each other's views on sex and likes and dislikes. Talk about if you need to go to a therapist. And if you do, promise each other that neither of you will judge if you do. Make your home a safe place for a healthy sex life.

I want to bring to our attention that there's a reason why divorce is so high in the church world just like the secular world. And I'm pretty sure it's not because of the great sex we're having.

I understand that this can be seen as a touchy subject. Professional help may be needed. There are many reasons why sex may not be the best in some marriages. There are situations of molestations, rape, medical issues and other very personal issues that can cause someone to feel embarrassed. Embarrassment and shame should not be hidden in the union of a man and woman. I want to encourage you to seek help for these issues. This book is a great start, but it may not be enough to conquer the past. It can help with your future but there are levels and layers that will take delicate hands to handle this sensitive situation. A healthy sex life is a wonderful thing to have and there's no reason for anyone to feel the shame or embarrassment of their past all their life. The mission for this chapter is to help and direct people to solutions that can help their marital bed be undefiled. I understand that for most people, they did not choose to approach sex from a place of shame. This was taught to them or absorbed by them through their upbringing. There is no reason to feel the shame or embarrassment, but if someone feels that way, they shouldn't be shamed for being a bit uncomfortable. Instead, we can help each other work through these thoughts and feelings and create a healthy relationship with our spouses.

This also applies to the spouse who may expect "more" as well. It is important for both partners to listen and be open-minded to have a healthy sex life. But as a disclosure, I'm not telling couples to turn into porn stars, I'm just saying be open-minded to what your spouse needs from you and why they need it. I was filled with a lot of lust early as a kid, and mentally I believed that sex could fix a lot of problems. I eventually learned that there is a line between right and wrong, too much and not enough in marriage. Sex is an important aspect of a healthy romantic relationship, but it cannot fix the problems that may have been created by early unwanted exposure to things like pornography. God isn't going to judge married people. Enjoy yourselves, work on your marriage, support one another, console each other, and have fun.

"Marriage is honorable among all, and the bed undefiled; but fornicators and adulterers God will judge." *(Hebrews 13:4 NKJV)*

Open Sesame

IN CONCLUSION

As we have come to the end of these book, let this be the beginning and continuation of a healthy lifestyle with new ways and techniques to make your relationship better. Marriage is a good thing, but it takes work¬—work you can do as long as you try without giving up. I hope you have enjoyed this journey and that you continue to walk out the plans God has for you. It has been placed on my heart to pray for you and to invite you into the family of God if you are not already a part of it. All you have to say is "Lord Jesus, I repent of my sins, come into my heart, I make you my Lord and Savior."

My brother or sister, if you prayed that prayer, I believe you have just been born again. Now, all you need to do is get into a Bible-base church that suits your taste and keep God first place in your life. I'm proud of you. Keep moving forward.

— Benjamin D. Author

www.ingramcontent.com/pod-product-compliance
Lightning Source LLC
Chambersburg PA
CBHW061508040426
42450CB00008B/1524